THE DAWN OR THE DUSK

NORIAN LOVE

Editing by John Briggs

ISBN-13: 9798631381285

To the reader thank you for your time
-No

A Student's Qualm

P assed every test,
    Learned every lesson.
Took every quiz,
Still you second guessin'
What we have is for real,
Maybe it's an excuse
Try to tell you the deal
But wondering. "What's the use?"
See, a part of me believes there is a you and I
But another part of me sees you're never satisfied...
See, you keep telling me we ought to be together
But anytime it rains you'd rather just change the weather
Hold on...
Question is, do you really want a man?
Or someone to constantly reassure you and hold your hand?
See, I can't keep up with those wandering eyes
Because it's human nature to think that they mean wandering thighs
But I ignore all that, no need for the speculation
Is this another test or you need this validation?

Looking at you telling me you feel similar energy
But in my peripheral see you sharing that chemistry
With anyone who you can make eye contact with
I feel like it's '95 and this some high school shit
But wait...
I could see it as a lesson to learn
'Cause if I'm constantly graded, maybe this is the midterm
But...
Sooner or later, you can mark my words
I'll get tired of these tests where there ain't no curve
See you're searching for perfection, so my 3.8
Ain't enough to pass this course I continue to take...
Teacher, teacher, maybe this is a mistake
I'll try to figure it out over this spring break
Take your notes, make your marks, do whatever it takes
I don't know if I'll be back after this spring break...

Breezy

H er cool...is irrefutable
      She was born half magnificent, half glorious
So they named her Gloria
Her familiarity with quality
An intrusion to the mundane
To call her beautiful insults her
To call her graceful is a tirade on her attributes
Her cool...sets standards
Angles haven't been this well designed
Art deviates from life anytime she speaks
Her cool...is marvelous
She is not cliché
I've watched her underachievements
They are miraculous
She is awe-inspiring
Her cool...an improvement on perfection
Eve, reborn
Her cool...

The Morning After, After

Dawn, the mistress of misery,
　　　Spews her acid, searing me back
Into the "reality," my love for her has tainted
It's all chemical now
Who notices the yelp of a wounded animal whose heart was caught in life's snare?
Bleeding across all of the facade humanity places...in primness and properly
Will the leakage continue?
Can I return to the robotic nature of man?
I've tasted oblivion on my fingertips
It's rank flavor still inside of my pores
The thoughts tear through as I put up my wall to
Force my rage back in the box of "I'm good, how are you?"
A lie I've exhausted...
But I purchased this rhetoric with good coin and in fair exchange you do the same
When we both know
There's a darkness consuming any passion I have left

The box is too small now
The walls will not erect themselves
My love letter to humanity
Good morning

Father to Son

I
f you could see yourself like I do, looking through my eyes
   Then you would understand why there are tears in my eyes
If I could explain how you've inspired me to just hold on
When I thought I wanted to give up
The thought of you made me strong
Father to son, son to father, one in the same
No matter where you are, in my heart you will remain
If you could see yourself, looking through my eyes
The greatest superhero on the earth
A parent's paradise
I know I'm hard on you at times
I never want to be
I wish all of your pain could some way be
Transferred to me
The only thing that I'm trying to do
Is make you better than me
So you impact the world with your greatness
And create history
If you could see yourself like I do, looking through my eyes

Then you would understand why there are tears in my eyes
I love you more than you ever will know
You'll never realize
Until you have your own son one day
And have tears in your eyes

Eudora

L ooking at you, girl, you beautiful
       Rose petals should be your cuticles
The way I'm holding you constantly feels like molding you
Knowing one day you'll leave me, no need in me controlling you
But truthfully, I love who you becoming
Every single day you evolving into that woman
That makes me feel confident this love affair is worth it
You'll never break my heart because I know that no one's perfect
I've been here a while...
My wife don't understand it
Ya momma will never get it
I can't even call it special
More chemically magnetic
I'm hoping somehow this lasts
So much trash in my past
Gallivanting with harlots
Whose scarlet letter would pass
I know that sometimes life can be a little crazy
But I never want you to be that kind of lady
And all the pillow talking that we doing

I know will probably ruin your chances of romances
With any brotha that's lazy
But...
If you leave me, just promise me you'll do better
'Cause on my life I'm prepared to support you forever
And it really don't matter what people think because you know I'll
be right here
I know you'll get it in a few years

3 A.M

Desires
     We all conceal the truth from one another
Hidden mysteries cradled in the witching hour
As lust takes a hold of your vessels, giving your all to one another
In the pretense of "this is just one night"
A relapse that happens over and over again
You reluctantly give in, willingly
To the fact you are in some ways egocentric
Gratifying man's sinful nature you disguise your
Return to a house of cards you claim to be whole
Until the question scrapes against your mind
Is this a palace or a prison?
When you so desperately seek escape
Sneaking past your cellmate
Hiding the residue of lust and guilt between your panty line,
Wondering,
Did he notice?
When truthfully a more pressing question,
With a more pertinent agenda

Escapes the forefront of your thoughts
While you were gone,
Where was he?
Desires...

Forward Play

Inserting my hyphenation into your monologue
   As you resist that painfully relaxing submission
I have you were I've wanted you to be
Where you knew I would one day live
And it's wonderful, no matter what happens
After the next cycle I'm alive at this very moment
WE are alive at this very moment
We speak in cataclysms

Designation

She is beauty...
  If she were a flower
She'd be a taboo rose.
If she were a horse
She'd be a thoroughbred.
If she were a painting
She'd be the Mona Lisa.
If she were a song
She'd be "Namia."
If she were a flavor
She'd be honey.
If she were a wine
She'd be Robert Foley Claret merlot.
Yet she is a woman
And so she is beauty

I Gotta Live with the Fact I Did You Wrong Forever

It's been a while since we talked and all that
   Reminiscing on how we kissed and how you kept me on track
Recalling how you used to taste like almond extract
Or how you used to leave me tender notes inside my backpack
I'm haunted by your memory and all the flashbacks
The time that we shared together made a hell of an impact
Wishing when I had your ear that I had told you all that
Wishing when I had your heart that I had loved you strong back
Wishing I had the sense to keep what we had intact
Each day without you now is a major setback
In fact, I often wish you'd decide to come back
Just knock on the door and tell me to help you unpack
That's just a fantasy that'll keep me side-tracked
All the things I said that hurt, I wish I could retract
Then "us" being together wouldn't seem so abstract
Called a couple times, you never seem to call back...
Wishing when I had your ear somehow I had told you all that
Wishing when I had your heart that I had loved you strong back

Love Song

I hear your song
It begins moving pieces of me around
Large chunks of who I've been made
Being polished
My bruises cleaned gently
My faith in tomorrow being restored
My regrets of yesterday being consoled
My belief that I no longer need to hold back...
Is being challenged
I want to kiss yesterday
And hold today
And love tomorrow
All because of this song
I see your canvas
As my own
And I want to paint.
A song shouldn't have that kind of effect
Yet
Every word
Chanted

Seems to come from my soul
Speaking for me
To a love departed
And I replay
Hoping you hear this tune
This time

23

Y ou told me you loved me but that was just a lie
     And I fell for your deception looking in your pretty eyes
I thought what we had was special and that you're one of a kind
I was infatuated with you; you were playing with my mind
I don't want to recollect this, but I guess it's finally time
Drinking, listening to Sade asking me "Is it a crime?"
Cause I know that you're a nickel yet I treat you like a dime
And that has nothing to do with your breast or your...
It's no question that you're attractive- let's just say that from the
start
But then factor in the "i" that is the malice in your heart
And if you add the two together, after that then u divide
Then the woman who's a "10" suddenly becomes a "5"
I was happy with that number cause my heart was damaged too
It was different, but convinced myself it complimented you
Till I saw all of the drama and the hell you'd take me through
You can't even be upset that I want no part of you
True I should have seen this coming Rico said you was a hoe
But that was back when we were younger I assumed that you
would grow

Introduced you to my son cause I thought you were the one
Plus you told me that you loved me...
Girl you told me that you loved me
Seemed to only say those words when you wanted something
from me
Wasn't long after you'd say them that you'd then manage to hurt me
Caught up in a vicious cycle,
We'd always seem to recycle
I'd keep giving you my heart,
Then you'd break it on arrival
But this time it's best I leave cause now I'm fighting for survival
My sanity's on the ledge, I'm really close to the edge
I'm finally out your snare and I honestly I don't care
What you're doing with your life, guess you took this as a dare
Cause you call me sometime later cause you "need to clear the air"
And I foolishly listen because I think I want to hear
And in a flash you undid everything I did to prepare
Cause you told me that you loved me
Girl you told me that you loved me...

Genesis

I was alone when I saw you, my future queen
   The most beautiful thing I'd ever seen- On this star filled eve
Didn't know what to call you
Didn't know what to say
The only thing I knew that I could do
Was pray that you'd stay
Running around paradise chasing you- I did whatever it takes
You were uncontrollable back then, made a couple mistakes
So I made them with you - what else could I do
Please understand all I was ever trying to do was protect you
So we had to leave ecstasy, but that was ok
Cause you were there right by my side so we were on our way
We were out in the wilderness, working hard all the time
No matter what we had to do for food and shelter, you didn't seem
to mind
Me and you against the whole damn world, just a man and wife
And on a night like the one where I met you- we created life
We made a beautiful family; it brought its pleasure and pain
But we endured it together no matter what and that's so hard to
attain

And I watched the wrinkles come over you as the time marched on
Holding hands until our golden years come and we both pass on
But before our next life time, there something you should know
I didn't regret anything along the way cause I love you so
If somehow I could go back- do it all over again
You and me in front of the fig tree, in the Garden of Eden
I would gladly pick the fig... and these words are true
Because the thing that is so misunderstood is...
My paradise is you

Nancy's Heartbeat

D o you ever think about me?
     I wonder all of the time
Am I ever at any moment?
A thought upon your mind
Do you ever wonder what I'm doing?
What's going on with me?
In conversations do I cross
Your mind currently?
I wish you thought about me
If only for a moment
And before that moment
Comes and goes
I wish that you would hold it
For just a second longer
Before it fleets away
And maybe then just maybe
You'd know I think of you each day

Through the Looking Glass

P eering at your complexity from the street corner
     How desperately I want to walk into this store
  I imagine myself purchasing,
  Like any shopper
  Who's made a fine decision
  The warmness of the lights
  The delight in smiling
  The pleasure
  Acquisition brings
  Even that of luxury items
  But I'm on the corner what seems like
  Miles
  Away
  From anything remotely like "to have and to hold"
  It's cold where I am
  Outside

Love's Meaning

I know the true meaning of love
   It's when you can't forget the time
And pleasure
You've spent with someone
Now that you can't spend it with them anymore
All you have left are memories of what was
I've spent an entire lifetime looking for what is love.
How does it feel?
Where will it take me?
And I've discovered that
It's not always what you put into it
Sometimes it's what you've taken away
And every now and again it is what remains
The things remembered,
The fleeting moments of time in which
We encompass mental photographs
Of the events transpired. When you no longer
Can hold the person the memories speak ballads to
Your heart

Moment of Adoration

I don't think you're ready for what I have to say
    I'm thinking about you almost every day
Yet I'm trying to find a better way
To tell you that I feel you like I never have
It just doesn't add up and I have *done* the math
Added us together, then divided all the obstacles
That makes us multiplying ourselves here impossible
Minus the nonsense we always equal great love
Maybe that's why it's the only thing I think of
Beautiful rouge lips pressed gently against mine
When it happens it feels like we have just paused time
Let's stop the world from moving if only for an hour
And call it daylight savings while we're in the shower
Pardon my boldness but everything about you
Is a requisite for me not wanting to live without you
I won't go into detail, just using my common senses
Infatuated by your design, the mirror is your compliment
And I'm so confident that my words won't equate much
Nothing I couldn't express through a mate's touch

So I'll adore you with my lips and know I'm sincere
That I'm thankful every moment that you spend here

Exes

W hen I was young, I dated *Fun*
      I met her in high school
She was all about the good time
Immature but yet so cool
Fat ass, tongue ring,
Man, she was so fine
I'd love to spend my time with her
She helped me to unwind...

SEE, ME AND *FUN* HAD A FLING
    In the summer I would love her
Then we'd hook up in the spring
But after a couple years of going strong
I started to mature, sometimes thought of moving on
I still stuck with *Fun* despite all of our setbacks
'Cause anytime we'd hit the club, she'd always like that
Couple shots of Jägermeister, vodka, and all that
Fun wanted to party till I passed out or fall flat...

. . .

SENIOR YEAR I WAS GETTING MORE INTO ME
Started feeling *Fun's* home-girl *Complacency*
See, *Fun* was the same girl since tenth grade
Now we're in college,
Accumulating knowledge
Complacency made me feel secure in different ways
So about an hour before, on our graduation day
I told *Fun,* "I think it's best we go our separate ways."
She took it kinda hard, but I guess she understood
She wasn't really ready to evolve like she should
We still were off and on from time to time
A few late-night creeps and afterhours bump 'n grinds

MEANWHILE *COMPLACENCY* HAD ME FEELING GOOD
Wasn't official, our relationship was understood
Being with her, I felt like I truly didn't care
So smug, yet at times I felt so unaware...
She didn't love me, I think I was just something to do
I didn't mind, though, she was just something to screw
But as more time went on the more time we'd spend
Before I knew it, *Complacency* was my girlfriend
Didn't see it start, but I knew she had my heart
'Cause I told *Fun* that our creeping had to end
Me and *Complacency* started going steady
Never had to wait on her, she was always ready
But truthfully we never did too much of anything
Couldn't talk to her, thought she knew everything
My mother never liked her
Told me more than once I was becoming like her
I didn't care what Momma had to say
The way me and *Complacency* would lay...damn

COMPLACENCY WAS COOL WITH THE FACT I WAS HER MAN
She knew this girl named *Success* that she couldn't stand

27

"She thinks she all that, I can't stand that chick,"
"I don't ask for much, stay away from that bitch!"
When I first saw *Success*
I have to admit I was impressed
I was marveled by her swagger and her confidence
How so many different people gave her complements
To get to know her only seemed like common sense
I guess I thought *Complacency* was bitchin'
And not insecure about her lack of ambition
I guess to her it seemed kinda odd
That I worked for a month and met *Success* on the job

Success WAS A LADY, SHE WAS ALL ABOUT HER GRIND
Had a nice body, but an even sharper mind
The more I worked, the more I had to deal with *Success*
Started seeing *Complacency* less and less
I could tell that she was kinda stressed
She would call every now and then to second guess
My every action, where was I? When would I come home?
"I called an hour ago, where was your cell phone?"
I tried to tell her it was all inside her head,
But truthfully, I was letting *Success* in my bed
I had fallen for her, *Complacency* was a thing of the past
She just wanted to chill too much, I was growing too fast
She finally had enough, said she was stopping by
She wanted to talk to me she told me this was goodbye
Said, "It's over," we broke up, she could tell I was cheating
She packed her bags same night, told me she was leaving
Said she wasn't stupid, she knew I was having sex
And she wasn't sure with who, but it smelled like *Success*
So from that moment, *Complacency* left me
I didn't really care, me and *Success* had chemistry
I thought her and I would be, so I didn't mind
She kinda stroked my ego, my love was blind
She had me dressing in nicer clothes

I got compliments, it seemed she liked those
I couldn't lie, I was feeling this
Success was a freak, such an exhibitionist
Turned her to know that other women were jockin'
Seemed she loved me harder when people were watchin'
Yet *Success* had a bunch of different problems
But I was into her, so I thought that I could solve them
I used to love her so constantly
For a while...I really thought she belonged to me
Didn't know I was just one of many more
Much too elegant for me to call her a whore
Damn...I guess I really couldn't trip
From the start, it was an open relationship
But I guess I thought *Success* was my woman
I f***ed her every day, so *Success* kept comin'
She told me she didn't want to settle down
She was bisexual, yeah, *Success,* she got around
She was too much to woman settle down with one man
At that age it was hard for me to understand
So I had to move on, as bad as I wanted *Success*
She came with heartbreak, envy, and plenty of stress

Success had a cousin named *Happiness*
They were just alike, but she seemed more delicate
We used to talk sometimes, she used to get so intricate
It didn't take me long for me and her to get intimate
I really liked her, but noticed she was hard to find
I used to see her when I was going out with *Fun* sometimes
Success was cool, but when was with her I felt alone
I thought Happiness could turn a house into a home
She kinda seemed like she'd make a good girlfriend
I didn't know her well, she was hard to comprehend
See, *Happiness* would come and go
Didn't know if that meant that she was a hoe
I didn't want another girl that got around like *Success*

29

Since they were related, that was the case, I guess
But I was wrong, what I didn't seem to understand
Was that *Happiness* just needed a one-woman man
And she heard some things *Complacency* had said
That made her wonder, if I just wanted to get ahead
Job, I told her I was looking for a woman
To help me in my life to complement what I was becoming
And for her there wasn't nothing in the would I wouldn't do
I'd even cater to her secret desire for Jimmy Choos
See, *Happiness* was pretty with no makeup
The catalyst for me and *Success* to start to break up
We started dating exclusively, just her and me
And shortly after that I asked her to move into my home
I had never felt this intense about anything
I wanted to give this girl a wedding ring
She had all *Success* had to offer, just a bit of *Fun*
Complacency's consistency, this girl was the one
She was all that I would want, I would need
So imagine her surprise when she caught me with *Greed*
She was built like *Success,* but nowhere near as classy
I saw her on the DL 'cause she was kind of trashy
Greed was a gold digger, no doubt
She only wanted more, never wanted to hold out
She was like a monster, she was always jealous
I took it as ambition that she was just overzealous
Should've listened to my fellas
When they told me that they'd had her and she always wanted
betta
I lost it all behind *Greed,* I thought of her as different
But to *Greed* all nature was truly insufficient
When *Happiness* found out, she told me to hold her
One last time before she finally said that it was over
"See, you had it all and you still wanted more."
"How long have you been dealing with *Greed*...that whore?"
I told her, "Baby, I'm sorry, I messed up badly."
I asked her to forgive me, but she responded sadly,

"I stayed for you to be a better person"
"And you were, or appeared to be, least that's what I'm learning"
"I really thought we enjoyed our living"
"I thought we had it all, but hell, who am I kidding?"
"Now I understand you're just like any other man."
"But as hard as I try, I really can't comprehend."
"We had it all. I'm not even mad at *Greed*."
"Or even you. I guess I'm really mad at me."
"I guess to sum it up, we're through."
"You can look for me, but I'll never come after you."

When I asked her what she meant, she said, "It's all in your pursuit."

Damn, I wish I would've listened
She kissed me one last time and then went missing
Tried to find her, but she's good at hiding
Didn't have time for me, she knew I had been lying
As far as it goes, *Greed,* that man-eating heifer
Left me the same day for someone who seemed better
Damn...now I'm living with *Regret*
Longing for the days I was living with *Happiness*

Nothing Left

So much to talk about
    Nothing to say at all
Starting to wonder what
Was the reason I called
I want to say I'm sorry
I hope you're OK
I wish you were right here
Right beside me
I had all these chances
All of these moments
I squandered them then
I wasted atonement
For that I must accept
The wrongs that I've done
By losing your trust
Our love was undone

Puppet Master

M y heart was your plaything
You picked me up
You tinkered on occasion
Sometimes effortlessly
Sometimes endlessly
Intensely
Then one day it was now and again
Lately...not at all
My clairvoyance now
Is a nightmarish dream
It pains me to think how
I enjoy puppeteering
For you...
I can't commit to walk
Away from this
For as much as I should leave
I'm hoping you pass by this shelf
Again
Frightens me to know that

My heart was...
Is...
Your plaything
To become aware
Is a nightmarish dream

Rag Doll

Y ou've taken the time we've spent together and discarded it
    Like a used, worthless
Rag doll.
The kisses
The joy
The sorrow as well
The intenseness
All of my adoration
Crumpled
By your hands and
Rejected.
Am I to believe that now you
Are not ready to move on without me?
Your footsteps
Have already been taken
Yet I stand where
You left me
My love
You left it

Abandoned
Like a used, worthless
Rag doll.

Satin

I touch satin every time
   I feel ecstasy with every breath
Hard to know the start or end
It's texture, life, or death?
How did satin get its name?
I wonder all the time
Buried in its essence now
I lose all sense of time
Was satin crafted carefully?
By the hands of god
Or was satin Satan's garment
And I should keep it by my guard?
However satin got its name
It must've taken it from you
Laying in your warmth right now
Only confirms this thought is true

The Scent of Forever

You lay in my arms...
          Nothing
Everything
Matters more
Or less
Kissing creates entire universes
Tomorrow and yesterday
Embrangled in one another
If passion weren't so minuscule a verb
I'd refer to our work as an act of it
I hold you in my dreams
And forget you in my nightmares
Tomorrow and yesterday
Embrangled in one another
Nothing
Matters more
Or less...

Soul Mate

This isn't something from the depths of my mind
    This is
This is something for this moment in time
This is
This is something that is somewhat sublime
This is
This is something from this woman of mine
The way she writes now, think she's reaching her prime
It's me and her forever, it's predestined design
The love that we share is strong; it's the tie that will bind
I used her for so long, she constantly held on
The only one who was there throughout my turbulent times
Helped me organize my thoughts, even put them into rhyme
She went deep into the tunnel in the heat of the night
Said she loved me, told me it will all be alright
She said she knew I was in pain, she understood my plight
Told me to hold her, showed me how to get up and fight
We wrote out of tunnel vision, started to see the light
When I was vision-less, she was there to give me insight
Convinced me not to use a sword; she had mightier might

She apprehended my fears
Consolidated my tears
She asked me why I felt like I could not be on top
Asked why I came this far and now was willing to stop
I told her how everyone told me how much I'd changed
How everyone misunderstood me and thought I was strange
She cut me off and said, "Yeah, damn right you've changed."
"Does it make sense to work this hard to stay the same?"
She told me she could tell that I was feeling the stress
And that's a part of the peril when you're achieving success
She told me to just keep moving forward nevertheless
Keep fighting, and work when all my enemies rest
She said keep holding onto her, just keep giving my all
For every Jesus there's Judas
For every Cesar, there's Brutus
For every triumph, there's someone who will pray for your fall
For every Kennedy, Malcolm X, for every King
There are conspirators, eager to put a hole in your dream
For every moment in life you try to strive for success
There's someone there to block you or to mock you at best
She explained to me, "Success is just like suicide."
"If at first you succeed, then prepare to be crucified."
After we talked, she quietly removed that block
And told me to use her, and so I started to—nonstop
And I fell in love with holding her all over again
I've known her since grade school, guess we've always been friends
She reminded me to smile more, like when I was a kid
And I was embarrassed of the silly things that she and I did
Like the time my mother caught us flirting in an intimate way
My interpretation of heaven was playing when I was seven
With my little baby brother 'bout to be born any day
And we wrote about it all, guess I kind of knew then
That we had something special, but I tried to pretend
Over the years I watched her grow, she became so strong
Blossomed became attractive, she could do no wrong
Made me express my bitterness, my unrest, and regrets

But also helped me scribe my joy and my love I couldn't forget
She's my one and only, now I'm married to her
When I die I hope my wife makes sure I'm buried with her
So if heaven really is what I described as a child
I'll be holding her, loving the way she makes me smile.

The Dawn or the Dusk

S hould I trust your actions at dusk?
   Or believe in your words at dawn?
At dusk you hold me
Caress me gingerly
Intimately
I wonder what will you
Have in store for me right before sunrise?
If anything at all...
Love is ambiguous that way
Is your love at dawn
The same love at dusk?
Too hard to tell apart
For they look so identical
On the surface.
I need to know...
Which one is undyingly true?
You call me by name at dusk
I only ask you to *call* me at dawn
Should I believe what you say to me in the twilight?
As we lay intermingled

Clinching,
Overwhelmed,
Consumed by one another's fury?
Should I give my strength, my forethoughts
My weakness?
Or should I wait until the dawn?
Will you still be overwhelmed by me then?
Will your every sense remain with me?
Within me...
Which one is *your* love?
The Dawn or
The Dusk?
Which one should I trust?

Nuclear Family

❧❦❧

I wish I was appreciated a little more
    I wish what I just wrote was a metaphor...
Neither one of us can remember what we're fighting for
Me & you, Sun Tzu in the art of war
Or
I wish we could show some remorse
And not be plaintiff, nor defendant inside this divorce
It's unfortunate that we had to choose this recourse
We're supposed to work things out, for better or worse
Yet we're sitting here talking to lawyers, expressing hate
Paying people who do know us to try to communicate
Everything that we've been through, getting it misconstrued
With both of them trying to win it's ultimately us who lose
Casue we ain't even speaking, You ask the kids who I'm seeing
I'm asking them if you have company on the weekend
And they're just sitting here thinking "I wish they'd just be together"
So they would quit asking us all the things they could ask each other
They're starting to feel the pressure; we're giving them all our pain

I'm talking reckless about you; you're calling me out of my name
Pawns inside of our game, we're just making them colder
To their questions we respond, "You'll understand when you're
older."
Now guarded with their emotions, we're teaching them how to lie
And teaching them how to fight, and now we're wondering why
Their relationships with their spouses aren't working out
They'd rather just do without, or rather just scream and shout
The irony is, now they're adults and they have kids
And like hypocrites we both them to "work things out"

Moonwalker

I f I could hold you just a while longer
I'd find a way to let you know
Every part of me, in every way
Never wants to let you go

IF I COULD SEE YOU DANCE AGAIN
To see you take your stride
I'd watch you through my tear-filled
Eyes my heart flowing with pride

TO HEAR YOU SING YOUR MELODIES
To hear you strike your chord
Would bear me such enchantment
I'd spend my existence in applaud

FOR YOU ALL THESE THINGS I'D DO

And do so happily
For none of it could ever compare
To the joy you've given to me

Fairy Tale

I've wondered almost all my life
   If fairy tales were real
And through my trials and errors
I know now how I truly feel
I've waited in my castle, hoping to one day meet a prince
One with charisma, charm, and poise and intelligence
I've dreamed of how he'd slay the dragon or
Maybe be a frog
That I would meet and greet and kiss while sitting on a log
But every frog was just a frog
No magic in my kiss
And every dragon slayer always seemed to hit and miss
I soon realized that this prince probably wasn't real
Just a tale to tell a child, I understood the deal
And one day I met someone remarkably unique
Not a frog, no shining armor, but in every way complete
No magic wands, potions, or spells, he was there for me
Soon I grew to understand he just cared...for me
He asked me just to walk with him to places not yet seen

He didn't see me as a princess ...he saw me as a queen
I've heard so many fairy tales
Wondered when would mine be true
On this day I now realize
I found them all in you

Forged

I imagined you in grade school
    I dreamed of you at camp
I thought of you in junior high
I wondered at my senior prom
Were you standing in front of me?
But you weren't...
I questioned if you were real
I had so much more to learn
I looked for you in others
And found things out about myself
For better and worse.
And I looked for you again, you still weren't there
I thought I was ready, but still had more growing to do
And so I grew...into who you needed me to be
I realize now you were always looking for me
Like I for you.
And had you arrived any sooner. I would not have
Been ready—we both needed to be forged to make
Our happily ever after perfect in every way
For us.

The Rose

I wonder if someone will find me today and admire me for me
And not for what the world expects me to be
Not primed nor cut nor dressed with decorations all around
But as I am naturally, growing from the ground
Am I not beautiful, not pretty, just the way I am?
Or do I need a makeover to make you give a damn?
If I decline the gloss and shine, would you be offended?
Just used my natural scent and beauty, the way the lord intended.
Would that make me unglamorous, unimpressive in your view?
If that's the case, then my beauty was never meant for you.

The Unicorn

A s she walked down the aisle
        Her divinity
So familiar, yet authentic in every way
I thought to myself, "She has a historical beauty"
"Like that of Nefertiti"
"Or Pam Grier."
Someone whose beauty will or should be remembered throughout
time
    She had the confidence of Sheba
    The strength of Assata
    And the innocence of my first box of crayons
    To think me the stallion,
    Untamable,
    Never willing to back down.
    Always willing to walk my own way
    I've finally found something worth being cultivated for
    I've found something
    Someone
    Majestic enough to trail through all of my years
    Someone to defend, to admire

A love so rare and beautiful
Only a stallion should be allowed to walk alongside
I ask, what is more imperial that a stallion
But a unicorn? Wars have been waged over women like you
And I, like those men before me, will die trying to preserve
The beauty and radiance that you possess if you would just
Allow me to walk with you for the rest of my life

About the Author

Norian Love was born in Los Angeles, California, in 1979. He grew up in Houston, Texas, where he's lived for the last twenty years. While taking a short hiatus from working for Fortune 500 companies as a technology specialist, he rediscovered his passion for writing poetry and released his first book, *Theater of Pain*, which was critically acclaimed. The reception and momentum of this book sparked him to create his eagerly anticipated follow up, *Games of the Heart*, a few years later. The final installment of his poetic trilogy, *The Dawn or the Dusk* has recently been released and is already receiving praise as the best book in the series.

Also by Norian Love

Memories of Tomorrow Series

Theater of Pain (Book 1)

Games of the Heart (Book 2)

The Dawn or the Dusk (Book 3)

Novels

Money, Power & Sex: A Love Story

Seduction: A Money .Power & Sex Story

Autumn: A Love Story

Ronnie: A Money, Power & Sex Story

Donovan: A Money, Power & Sex Novella

Made in the USA
Coppell, TX
22 February 2024